To:

From:

Date:

Printed in Vietnam

DELIGHT YOURSELF IN THE LORD, AND HE WILL
GIVE YOU THE DESIRES OF YOUR HEART.

PSALM 37:4

IN YOU, O LORD, DO I PUT MY TRUST AND CONFIDENTLY TAKE REFUGE; LET ME NEVER BE PUT TO SHAME OR CONFUSION!

PSALM 71:1

"BE STRONG AND COURAGEOUS. . . . THE LORD
YOUR GOD WILL BE WITH YOU WHEREVER YOU GO."

JOSHUA 1:9

DEPEND ON THE LORD IN WHATEVER YOU DO,
AND YOUR PLANS WILL SUCCEED.

PROVERBS 16:3

SINCE WE HAVE BEEN JUSTIFIED THROUGH FAITH, WE HAVE PEACE WITH GOD THROUGH OUR LORD JESUS CHRIST.

ROMANS 5:1

THE LORD IS MY ROCK, MY FORTRESS AND MY DELIVERER;
MY GOD IS MY ROCK, IN WHOM I TAKE REFUGE.

PSALM 18:2

"IF ANYONE WOULD COME AFTER ME, LET HIM DENY HIMSELF AND TAKE UP HIS CROSS AND FOLLOW ME."

MATTHEW 16:24

THE WORD OF THE LORD IS RIGHT AND TRUE;
HE IS FAITHFUL IN ALL HE DOES.

PSALM 33:4

THE LORD IS MY STRENGTH AND SHIELD.
I TRUST HIM WITH ALL MY HEART.

PSALM 28:7

IN HIM WE HAVE REDEMPTION THROUGH HIS BLOOD, THE FORGIVENESS OF SINS, IN ACCORDANCE WITH THE RICHES OF GOD'S GRACE.

EPHESIANS 1:7

I TRUST IN YOUR UNFAILING LOVE. I WILL REJOICE BECAUSE YOU HAVE RESCUED ME. I WILL SING TO THE LORD BECAUSE HE IS GOOD TO ME.

PSALM 13:5-6

WALK IN THE WAY OF LOVE, JUST AS CHRIST LOVED US AND GAVE HIMSELF UP FOR US AS A FRAGRANT OFFERING AND SACRIFICE TO GOD.

EPHESIANS 5:2

"YOU WILL CALL ON ME AND COME AND PRAY TO ME,
AND I WILL LISTEN TO YOU. YOU WILL SEEK ME AND FIND
ME WHEN YOU SEEK ME WITH ALL YOUR HEART."

JEREMIAH 29:12-13

MY SOUL FINDS REST IN GOD;
MY SALVATION COMES FROM HIM.

PSALM 62:1

DELIGHT YOURSELF IN THE LORD, AND HE WILL
GIVE YOU THE DESIRES OF YOUR HEART.

PSALM 37:4

THE LORD IS MY LIGHT AND MY SALVATION—
WHOM SHALL I FEAR? THE LORD IS THE STRONGHOLD
OF MY LIFE—OF WHOM SHALL I BE AFRAID?

PSALM 27:1

THE LORD HIMSELF GOES BEFORE YOU AND WILL BE WITH YOU; HE WILL NEVER LEAVE YOU NOR FORSAKE YOU.

DEUTERONOMY 31:8

GOD IS WORKING IN YOU, GIVING YOU THE DESIRE
AND THE POWER TO DO WHAT PLEASES HIM.

PHILIPPIANS 2:13

I CAN DO EVERYTHING THROUGH CHRIST,
WHO GIVES ME STRENGTH.

PHILIPPIANS 4:13

IF YOU WANT TO KNOW WHAT GOD WANTS YOU TO DO, ASK HIM, AND HE WILL GLADLY TELL YOU.

JAMES 1:5

CREATE IN ME A PURE HEART, O GOD,
AND RENEW A STEADFAST SPIRIT WITHIN ME.

PSALM 51:10

IF ANYONE IS IN CHRIST, HE IS A NEW CREATION.
THE OLD HAS PASSED AWAY; BEHOLD, THE NEW HAS COME.

2 CORINTHIANS 5:17

CAST YOUR CARES ON THE LORD
AND HE WILL SUSTAIN YOU.

PSALM 55:22

THE LORD YOUR GOD IS IN YOUR MIDST, A MIGHTY ONE WHO WILL SAVE; HE WILL REJOICE OVER YOU WITH GLADNESS; HE WILL QUIET YOU BY HIS LOVE.

ZEPHANIAH 3:17

THE LORD IS TRUSTWORTHY IN ALL HE PROMISES AND FAITHFUL IN ALL HE DOES.

PSALM 145:13

IN YOU, O LORD, DO I PUT MY TRUST AND
CONFIDENTLY TAKE REFUGE; LET ME NEVER
BE PUT TO SHAME OR CONFUSION!

PSALM 71:1

"BE STRONG AND COURAGEOUS. . . . THE LORD
YOUR GOD WILL BE WITH YOU WHEREVER YOU GO."

JOSHUA 1:9

DEPEND ON THE LORD IN WHATEVER YOU DO,
AND YOUR PLANS WILL SUCCEED.

PROVERBS 16:3

SINCE WE HAVE BEEN JUSTIFIED THROUGH FAITH, WE HAVE PEACE WITH GOD THROUGH OUR LORD JESUS CHRIST.

ROMANS 5:1

THE LORD IS MY ROCK, MY FORTRESS AND MY DELIVERER;
MY GOD IS MY ROCK, IN WHOM I TAKE REFUGE.

PSALM 18:2

"IF ANYONE WOULD COME AFTER ME, LET HIM DENY HIMSELF AND TAKE UP HIS CROSS AND FOLLOW ME."

MATTHEW 16:24

THE WORD OF THE LORD IS RIGHT AND TRUE;
HE IS FAITHFUL IN ALL HE DOES.

PSALM 33:4

THE LORD IS MY STRENGTH AND SHIELD.
I TRUST HIM WITH ALL MY HEART.

PSALM 28:7

IN HIM WE HAVE REDEMPTION THROUGH HIS BLOOD, THE FORGIVENESS OF SINS, IN ACCORDANCE WITH THE RICHES OF GOD'S GRACE.

EPHESIANS 1:7

I TRUST IN YOUR UNFAILING LOVE. I WILL REJOICE BECAUSE YOU HAVE RESCUED ME. I WILL SING TO THE LORD BECAUSE HE IS GOOD TO ME.

PSALM 13:5-6

WALK IN THE WAY OF LOVE, JUST AS CHRIST LOVED US AND GAVE HIMSELF UP FOR US AS A FRAGRANT OFFERING AND SACRIFICE TO GOD.

EPHESIANS 5:2

"YOU WILL CALL ON ME AND COME AND PRAY TO ME, AND I WILL LISTEN TO YOU. YOU WILL SEEK ME AND FIND ME WHEN YOU SEEK ME WITH ALL YOUR HEART."

JEREMIAH 29:12-13

MY SOUL FINDS REST IN GOD;
MY SALVATION COMES FROM HIM.

PSALM 62:1

DELIGHT YOURSELF IN THE LORD, AND HE WILL
GIVE YOU THE DESIRES OF YOUR HEART.

PSALM 37:4

THE LORD IS MY LIGHT AND MY SALVATION—
WHOM SHALL I FEAR? THE LORD IS THE STRONGHOLD
OF MY LIFE—OF WHOM SHALL I BE AFRAID?

PSALM 27:1

THE LORD HIMSELF GOES BEFORE YOU AND WILL BE WITH YOU; HE WILL NEVER LEAVE YOU NOR FORSAKE YOU.

DEUTERONOMY 31:8

GOD IS WORKING IN YOU, GIVING YOU THE DESIRE
AND THE POWER TO DO WHAT PLEASES HIM.

PHILIPPIANS 2:13

I CAN DO EVERYTHING THROUGH CHRIST,
WHO GIVES ME STRENGTH.

PHILIPPIANS 4:13

IF YOU WANT TO KNOW WHAT GOD WANTS YOU
TO DO, ASK HIM, AND HE WILL GLADLY TELL YOU.

JAMES 1:5

CREATE IN ME A PURE HEART, O GOD,
AND RENEW A STEADFAST SPIRIT WITHIN ME.

PSALM 51:10

IF ANYONE IS IN CHRIST, HE IS A NEW CREATION.
THE OLD HAS PASSED AWAY; BEHOLD, THE NEW HAS COME.

2 CORINTHIANS 5:17

CAST YOUR CARES ON THE LORD
AND HE WILL SUSTAIN YOU.

PSALM 55:22

THE LORD YOUR GOD IS IN YOUR MIDST, A MIGHTY ONE WHO WILL SAVE; HE WILL REJOICE OVER YOU WITH GLADNESS; HE WILL QUIET YOU BY HIS LOVE.

ZEPHANIAH 3:17

THE LORD IS TRUSTWORTHY IN ALL HE PROMISES AND FAITHFUL IN ALL HE DOES.

PSALM 145:13

IN YOU, O LORD, DO I PUT MY TRUST AND CONFIDENTLY TAKE REFUGE; LET ME NEVER BE PUT TO SHAME OR CONFUSION!

PSALM 71:1

"BE STRONG AND COURAGEOUS. . . . THE LORD
YOUR GOD WILL BE WITH YOU WHEREVER YOU GO."

JOSHUA 1:9

DEPEND ON THE LORD IN WHATEVER YOU DO,
AND YOUR PLANS WILL SUCCEED.

PROVERBS 16:3

SINCE WE HAVE BEEN JUSTIFIED THROUGH
FAITH, WE HAVE PEACE WITH GOD THROUGH
OUR LORD JESUS CHRIST.

ROMANS 5:1

THE LORD IS MY ROCK, MY FORTRESS AND MY DELIVERER;
MY GOD IS MY ROCK, IN WHOM I TAKE REFUGE.

PSALM 18:2

"IF ANYONE WOULD COME AFTER ME, LET HIM DENY HIMSELF AND TAKE UP HIS CROSS AND FOLLOW ME."

MATTHEW 16:24

THE WORD OF THE LORD IS RIGHT AND TRUE;
HE IS FAITHFUL IN ALL HE DOES.

PSALM 33:4

THE LORD IS MY STRENGTH AND SHIELD.
I TRUST HIM WITH ALL MY HEART.

PSALM 28:7

IN HIM WE HAVE REDEMPTION THROUGH HIS BLOOD, THE FORGIVENESS OF SINS, IN ACCORDANCE WITH THE RICHES OF GOD'S GRACE.

EPHESIANS 1:7

I TRUST IN YOUR UNFAILING LOVE. I WILL REJOICE BECAUSE YOU HAVE RESCUED ME. I WILL SING TO THE LORD BECAUSE HE IS GOOD TO ME.

PSALM 13:5-6

WALK IN THE WAY OF LOVE, JUST AS CHRIST LOVED US AND GAVE HIMSELF UP FOR US AS A FRAGRANT OFFERING AND SACRIFICE TO GOD.

EPHESIANS 5:2

"YOU WILL CALL ON ME AND COME AND PRAY TO ME, AND I WILL LISTEN TO YOU. YOU WILL SEEK ME AND FIND ME WHEN YOU SEEK ME WITH ALL YOUR HEART."

JEREMIAH 29:12-13

MY SOUL FINDS REST IN GOD;
MY SALVATION COMES FROM HIM.

PSALM 62:1

DELIGHT YOURSELF IN THE LORD, AND HE WILL
GIVE YOU THE DESIRES OF YOUR HEART.

PSALM 37:4

THE LORD IS MY LIGHT AND MY SALVATION—
WHOM SHALL I FEAR? THE LORD IS THE STRONGHOLD
OF MY LIFE—OF WHOM SHALL I BE AFRAID?

PSALM 27:1

THE LORD HIMSELF GOES BEFORE YOU AND WILL BE WITH YOU; HE WILL NEVER LEAVE YOU NOR FORSAKE YOU.

DEUTERONOMY 31:8

GOD IS WORKING IN YOU, GIVING YOU THE DESIRE AND THE POWER TO DO WHAT PLEASES HIM.

PHILIPPIANS 2:13

I CAN DO EVERYTHING THROUGH CHRIST,
WHO GIVES ME STRENGTH.

PHILIPPIANS 4:13

IF YOU WANT TO KNOW WHAT GOD WANTS YOU
TO DO, ASK HIM, AND HE WILL GLADLY TELL YOU.

JAMES 1:5

CREATE IN ME A PURE HEART, O GOD,
AND RENEW A STEADFAST SPIRIT WITHIN ME.

PSALM 51:10

IF ANYONE IS IN CHRIST, HE IS A NEW CREATION.
THE OLD HAS PASSED AWAY; BEHOLD, THE NEW HAS COME.

2 CORINTHIANS 5:17

CAST YOUR CARES ON THE LORD
AND HE WILL SUSTAIN YOU.

PSALM 55:22

THE LORD YOUR GOD IS IN YOUR MIDST, A MIGHTY ONE WHO WILL SAVE; HE WILL REJOICE OVER YOU WITH GLADNESS; HE WILL QUIET YOU BY HIS LOVE.

ZEPHANIAH 3:17

THE LORD IS TRUSTWORTHY IN ALL HE PROMISES AND FAITHFUL IN ALL HE DOES.

PSALM 145:13

IN YOU, O LORD, DO I PUT MY TRUST AND CONFIDENTLY TAKE REFUGE; LET ME NEVER BE PUT TO SHAME OR CONFUSION!

PSALM 71:1

"BE STRONG AND COURAGEOUS. . . . THE LORD
YOUR GOD WILL BE WITH YOU WHEREVER YOU GO."

JOSHUA 1:9

DEPEND ON THE LORD IN WHATEVER YOU DO,
AND YOUR PLANS WILL SUCCEED.

PROVERBS 16:3

SINCE WE HAVE BEEN JUSTIFIED THROUGH
FAITH, WE HAVE PEACE WITH GOD THROUGH
OUR LORD JESUS CHRIST.

ROMANS 5:1

THE LORD IS MY ROCK, MY FORTRESS AND MY DELIVERER;
MY GOD IS MY ROCK, IN WHOM I TAKE REFUGE.

PSALM 18:2

"IF ANYONE WOULD COME AFTER ME, LET HIM DENY
HIMSELF AND TAKE UP HIS CROSS AND FOLLOW ME."

MATTHEW 16:24

THE WORD OF THE LORD IS RIGHT AND TRUE;
HE IS FAITHFUL IN ALL HE DOES.

PSALM 33:4

THE LORD IS MY STRENGTH AND SHIELD.
I TRUST HIM WITH ALL MY HEART.

PSALM 28:7

IN HIM WE HAVE REDEMPTION THROUGH HIS
BLOOD, THE FORGIVENESS OF SINS, IN ACCORDANCE
WITH THE RICHES OF GOD'S GRACE.

EPHESIANS 1:7

I TRUST IN YOUR UNFAILING LOVE. I WILL REJOICE BECAUSE YOU HAVE RESCUED ME. I WILL SING TO THE LORD BECAUSE HE IS GOOD TO ME.

PSALM 13:5-6

WALK IN THE WAY OF LOVE, JUST AS CHRIST LOVED US AND GAVE HIMSELF UP FOR US AS A FRAGRANT OFFERING AND SACRIFICE TO GOD.

EPHESIANS 5:2

"YOU WILL CALL ON ME AND COME AND PRAY TO ME, AND I WILL LISTEN TO YOU. YOU WILL SEEK ME AND FIND ME WHEN YOU SEEK ME WITH ALL YOUR HEART."

JEREMIAH 29:12-13

MY SOUL FINDS REST IN GOD;
MY SALVATION COMES FROM HIM.

PSALM 62:1

DELIGHT YOURSELF IN THE LORD, AND HE WILL
GIVE YOU THE DESIRES OF YOUR HEART.

PSALM 37:4

THE LORD IS MY LIGHT AND MY SALVATION—
WHOM SHALL I FEAR? THE LORD IS THE STRONGHOLD
OF MY LIFE—OF WHOM SHALL I BE AFRAID?

PSALM 27:1

THE LORD HIMSELF GOES BEFORE YOU AND WILL BE WITH YOU; HE WILL NEVER LEAVE YOU NOR FORSAKE YOU.

DEUTERONOMY 31:8

GOD IS WORKING IN YOU, GIVING YOU THE DESIRE
AND THE POWER TO DO WHAT PLEASES HIM.

PHILIPPIANS 2:13

I CAN DO EVERYTHING THROUGH CHRIST,
WHO GIVES ME STRENGTH.

PHILIPPIANS 4:13

IF YOU WANT TO KNOW WHAT GOD WANTS YOU
TO DO, ASK HIM, AND HE WILL GLADLY TELL YOU.

JAMES 1:5

CREATE IN ME A PURE HEART, O GOD,
AND RENEW A STEADFAST SPIRIT WITHIN ME.

PSALM 51:10

IF ANYONE IS IN CHRIST, HE IS A NEW CREATION.
THE OLD HAS PASSED AWAY; BEHOLD, THE NEW HAS COME.

2 CORINTHIANS 5:17

CAST YOUR CARES ON THE LORD
AND HE WILL SUSTAIN YOU.

PSALM 55:22

THE LORD YOUR GOD IS IN YOUR MIDST, A MIGHTY ONE WHO WILL SAVE; HE WILL REJOICE OVER YOU WITH GLADNESS; HE WILL QUIET YOU BY HIS LOVE.

ZEPHANIAH 3:17

THE LORD IS TRUSTWORTHY IN ALL HE PROMISES AND FAITHFUL IN ALL HE DOES.

PSALM 145:13

IN YOU, O LORD, DO I PUT MY TRUST AND
CONFIDENTLY TAKE REFUGE; LET ME NEVER
BE PUT TO SHAME OR CONFUSION!

PSALM 71:1

"BE STRONG AND COURAGEOUS. . . . THE LORD YOUR GOD WILL BE WITH YOU WHEREVER YOU GO."

JOSHUA 1:9

DEPEND ON THE LORD IN WHATEVER YOU DO,
AND YOUR PLANS WILL SUCCEED.

PROVERBS 16:3

SINCE WE HAVE BEEN JUSTIFIED THROUGH FAITH, WE HAVE PEACE WITH GOD THROUGH OUR LORD JESUS CHRIST.

ROMANS 5:1

THE LORD IS MY ROCK, MY FORTRESS AND MY DELIVERER;
MY GOD IS MY ROCK, IN WHOM I TAKE REFUGE.

PSALM 18:2

"IF ANYONE WOULD COME AFTER ME, LET HIM DENY HIMSELF AND TAKE UP HIS CROSS AND FOLLOW ME."

MATTHEW 16:24

THE WORD OF THE LORD IS RIGHT AND TRUE;
HE IS FAITHFUL IN ALL HE DOES.

PSALM 33:4

THE LORD IS MY STRENGTH AND SHIELD.
I TRUST HIM WITH ALL MY HEART.

PSALM 28:7

IN HIM WE HAVE REDEMPTION THROUGH HIS BLOOD, THE FORGIVENESS OF SINS, IN ACCORDANCE WITH THE RICHES OF GOD'S GRACE.

EPHESIANS 1:7

I TRUST IN YOUR UNFAILING LOVE. I WILL REJOICE
BECAUSE YOU HAVE RESCUED ME. I WILL SING TO
THE LORD BECAUSE HE IS GOOD TO ME.

PSALM 13:5-6

WALK IN THE WAY OF LOVE, JUST AS CHRIST LOVED US AND GAVE HIMSELF UP FOR US AS A FRAGRANT OFFERING AND SACRIFICE TO GOD.

EPHESIANS 5:2

"YOU WILL CALL ON ME AND COME AND PRAY TO ME,
AND I WILL LISTEN TO YOU. YOU WILL SEEK ME AND FIND
ME WHEN YOU SEEK ME WITH ALL YOUR HEART."

JEREMIAH 29:12-13

MY SOUL FINDS REST IN GOD;
MY SALVATION COMES FROM HIM.

PSALM 62:1

DELIGHT YOURSELF IN THE LORD, AND HE WILL
GIVE YOU THE DESIRES OF YOUR HEART.

PSALM 37:4

THE LORD IS MY LIGHT AND MY SALVATION—
WHOM SHALL I FEAR? THE LORD IS THE STRONGHOLD
OF MY LIFE—OF WHOM SHALL I BE AFRAID?

PSALM 27:1

THE LORD HIMSELF GOES BEFORE YOU AND WILL BE WITH YOU; HE WILL NEVER LEAVE YOU NOR FORSAKE YOU.

DEUTERONOMY 31:8

GOD IS WORKING IN YOU, GIVING YOU THE DESIRE
AND THE POWER TO DO WHAT PLEASES HIM.

PHILIPPIANS 2:13

I CAN DO EVERYTHING THROUGH CHRIST,
WHO GIVES ME STRENGTH.

PHILIPPIANS 4:13

IF YOU WANT TO KNOW WHAT GOD WANTS YOU
TO DO, ASK HIM, AND HE WILL GLADLY TELL YOU.

JAMES 1:5

CREATE IN ME A PURE HEART, O GOD,
AND RENEW A STEADFAST SPIRIT WITHIN ME.

PSALM 51:10

IF ANYONE IS IN CHRIST, HE IS A NEW CREATION.
THE OLD HAS PASSED AWAY; BEHOLD, THE NEW HAS COME.

2 CORINTHIANS 5:17

CAST YOUR CARES ON THE LORD
AND HE WILL SUSTAIN YOU.

PSALM 55:22

THE LORD YOUR GOD IS IN YOUR MIDST, A MIGHTY ONE WHO WILL SAVE; HE WILL REJOICE OVER YOU WITH GLADNESS; HE WILL QUIET YOU BY HIS LOVE.

ZEPHANIAH 3:17

THE LORD IS TRUSTWORTHY IN ALL HE
PROMISES AND FAITHFUL IN ALL HE DOES.

PSALM 145:13

IN YOU, O LORD, DO I PUT MY TRUST AND CONFIDENTLY TAKE REFUGE; LET ME NEVER BE PUT TO SHAME OR CONFUSION!

PSALM 71:1

"BE STRONG AND COURAGEOUS. . . . THE LORD
YOUR GOD WILL BE WITH YOU WHEREVER YOU GO."

JOSHUA 1:9

DEPEND ON THE LORD IN WHATEVER YOU DO,
AND YOUR PLANS WILL SUCCEED.

PROVERBS 16:3

SINCE WE HAVE BEEN JUSTIFIED THROUGH
FAITH, WE HAVE PEACE WITH GOD THROUGH
OUR LORD JESUS CHRIST.

ROMANS 5:1

THE LORD IS MY ROCK, MY FORTRESS AND MY DELIVERER;
MY GOD IS MY ROCK, IN WHOM I TAKE REFUGE.

PSALM 18:2

"IF ANYONE WOULD COME AFTER ME, LET HIM DENY HIMSELF AND TAKE UP HIS CROSS AND FOLLOW ME."

MATTHEW 16:24

THE WORD OF THE LORD IS RIGHT AND TRUE;
HE IS FAITHFUL IN ALL HE DOES.

PSALM 33:4

THE LORD IS MY STRENGTH AND SHIELD.
I TRUST HIM WITH ALL MY HEART.

PSALM 28:7

IN HIM WE HAVE REDEMPTION THROUGH HIS BLOOD, THE FORGIVENESS OF SINS, IN ACCORDANCE WITH THE RICHES OF GOD'S GRACE.

EPHESIANS 1:7

I TRUST IN YOUR UNFAILING LOVE. I WILL REJOICE
BECAUSE YOU HAVE RESCUED ME. I WILL SING TO
THE LORD BECAUSE HE IS GOOD TO ME.

PSALM 13:5-6

WALK IN THE WAY OF LOVE, JUST AS CHRIST LOVED US AND GAVE HIMSELF UP FOR US AS A FRAGRANT OFFERING AND SACRIFICE TO GOD.

EPHESIANS 5:2

"YOU WILL CALL ON ME AND COME AND PRAY TO ME, AND I WILL LISTEN TO YOU. YOU WILL SEEK ME AND FIND ME WHEN YOU SEEK ME WITH ALL YOUR HEART."

JEREMIAH 29:12-13

MY SOUL FINDS REST IN GOD;
MY SALVATION COMES FROM HIM.

PSALM 62:1

DELIGHT YOURSELF IN THE LORD, AND HE WILL
GIVE YOU THE DESIRES OF YOUR HEART.

PSALM 37:4

THE LORD IS MY LIGHT AND MY SALVATION—
WHOM SHALL I FEAR? THE LORD IS THE STRONGHOLD
OF MY LIFE—OF WHOM SHALL I BE AFRAID?

PSALM 27:1

THE LORD HIMSELF GOES BEFORE YOU AND WILL BE WITH YOU; HE WILL NEVER LEAVE YOU NOR FORSAKE YOU.

DEUTERONOMY 31:8

GOD IS WORKING IN YOU, GIVING YOU THE DESIRE
AND THE POWER TO DO WHAT PLEASES HIM.

PHILIPPIANS 2:13

I CAN DO EVERYTHING THROUGH CHRIST,
WHO GIVES ME STRENGTH.

PHILIPPIANS 4:13

IF YOU WANT TO KNOW WHAT GOD WANTS YOU
TO DO, ASK HIM, AND HE WILL GLADLY TELL YOU.

JAMES 1:5

CREATE IN ME A PURE HEART, O GOD,
AND RENEW A STEADFAST SPIRIT WITHIN ME.

PSALM 51:10

IF ANYONE IS IN CHRIST, HE IS A NEW CREATION.
THE OLD HAS PASSED AWAY; BEHOLD, THE NEW HAS COME.

2 CORINTHIANS 5:17

CAST YOUR CARES ON THE LORD
AND HE WILL SUSTAIN YOU.

PSALM 55:22

THE LORD YOUR GOD IS IN YOUR MIDST, A MIGHTY ONE
WHO WILL SAVE; HE WILL REJOICE OVER YOU WITH
GLADNESS; HE WILL QUIET YOU BY HIS LOVE.

ZEPHANIAH 3:17

THE LORD IS TRUSTWORTHY IN ALL HE
PROMISES AND FAITHFUL IN ALL HE DOES.

PSALM 145:13

IN YOU, O LORD, DO I PUT MY TRUST AND CONFIDENTLY TAKE REFUGE; LET ME NEVER BE PUT TO SHAME OR CONFUSION!

PSALM 71:1

"BE STRONG AND COURAGEOUS. . . . THE LORD YOUR GOD WILL BE WITH YOU WHEREVER YOU GO."

JOSHUA 1:9

DEPEND ON THE LORD IN WHATEVER YOU DO,
AND YOUR PLANS WILL SUCCEED.

PROVERBS 16:3

SINCE WE HAVE BEEN JUSTIFIED THROUGH FAITH, WE HAVE PEACE WITH GOD THROUGH OUR LORD JESUS CHRIST.

ROMANS 5:1

THE LORD IS MY ROCK, MY FORTRESS AND MY DELIVERER;
MY GOD IS MY ROCK, IN WHOM I TAKE REFUGE.

PSALM 18:2

"IF ANYONE WOULD COME AFTER ME, LET HIM DENY HIMSELF AND TAKE UP HIS CROSS AND FOLLOW ME."

MATTHEW 16:24

THE WORD OF THE LORD IS RIGHT AND TRUE;
HE IS FAITHFUL IN ALL HE DOES.

PSALM 33:4

THE LORD IS MY STRENGTH AND SHIELD.
I TRUST HIM WITH ALL MY HEART.

PSALM 28:7

IN HIM WE HAVE REDEMPTION THROUGH HIS
BLOOD, THE FORGIVENESS OF SINS, IN ACCORDANCE
WITH THE RICHES OF GOD'S GRACE.

EPHESIANS 1:7

I TRUST IN YOUR UNFAILING LOVE. I WILL REJOICE
BECAUSE YOU HAVE RESCUED ME. I WILL SING TO
THE LORD BECAUSE HE IS GOOD TO ME.

PSALM 13:5-6

WALK IN THE WAY OF LOVE, JUST AS CHRIST LOVED US AND GAVE HIMSELF UP FOR US AS A FRAGRANT OFFERING AND SACRIFICE TO GOD.

EPHESIANS 5:2

"YOU WILL CALL ON ME AND COME AND PRAY TO ME,
AND I WILL LISTEN TO YOU. YOU WILL SEEK ME AND FIND
ME WHEN YOU SEEK ME WITH ALL YOUR HEART."

JEREMIAH 29:12-13

MY SOUL FINDS REST IN GOD;
MY SALVATION COMES FROM HIM.

PSALM 62:1

DELIGHT YOURSELF IN THE LORD, AND HE WILL
GIVE YOU THE DESIRES OF YOUR HEART.

PSALM 37:4

THE LORD IS MY LIGHT AND MY SALVATION—
WHOM SHALL I FEAR? THE LORD IS THE STRONGHOLD
OF MY LIFE—OF WHOM SHALL I BE AFRAID?

PSALM 27:1

THE LORD HIMSELF GOES BEFORE YOU AND WILL BE WITH YOU; HE WILL NEVER LEAVE YOU NOR FORSAKE YOU.

DEUTERONOMY 31:8

GOD IS WORKING IN YOU, GIVING YOU THE DESIRE AND THE POWER TO DO WHAT PLEASES HIM.

PHILIPPIANS 2:13

I CAN DO EVERYTHING THROUGH CHRIST,
WHO GIVES ME STRENGTH.

PHILIPPIANS 4:13

IF YOU WANT TO KNOW WHAT GOD WANTS YOU
TO DO, ASK HIM, AND HE WILL GLADLY TELL YOU.

JAMES 1:5

CREATE IN ME A PURE HEART, O GOD,
AND RENEW A STEADFAST SPIRIT WITHIN ME.

PSALM 51:10

IF ANYONE IS IN CHRIST, HE IS A NEW CREATION.
THE OLD HAS PASSED AWAY; BEHOLD, THE NEW HAS COME.

2 CORINTHIANS 5:17

CAST YOUR CARES ON THE LORD
AND HE WILL SUSTAIN YOU.

PSALM 55:22

THE LORD YOUR GOD IS IN YOUR MIDST, A MIGHTY ONE WHO WILL SAVE; HE WILL REJOICE OVER YOU WITH GLADNESS; HE WILL QUIET YOU BY HIS LOVE.

ZEPHANIAH 3:17

THE LORD IS TRUSTWORTHY IN ALL HE PROMISES AND FAITHFUL IN ALL HE DOES.

PSALM 145:13

IN YOU, O LORD, DO I PUT MY TRUST AND CONFIDENTLY TAKE REFUGE; LET ME NEVER BE PUT TO SHAME OR CONFUSION!

PSALM 71:1

"BE STRONG AND COURAGEOUS. . . . THE LORD
YOUR GOD WILL BE WITH YOU WHEREVER YOU GO."

JOSHUA 1:9

DEPEND ON THE LORD IN WHATEVER YOU DO,
AND YOUR PLANS WILL SUCCEED.

PROVERBS 16:3

SINCE WE HAVE BEEN JUSTIFIED THROUGH FAITH, WE HAVE PEACE WITH GOD THROUGH OUR LORD JESUS CHRIST.

ROMANS 5:1

THE LORD IS MY ROCK, MY FORTRESS AND MY DELIVERER;
MY GOD IS MY ROCK, IN WHOM I TAKE REFUGE.

PSALM 18:2

"IF ANYONE WOULD COME AFTER ME, LET HIM DENY HIMSELF AND TAKE UP HIS CROSS AND FOLLOW ME."

MATTHEW 16:24

THE WORD OF THE LORD IS RIGHT AND TRUE;
HE IS FAITHFUL IN ALL HE DOES.

PSALM 33:4

THE LORD IS MY STRENGTH AND SHIELD.
I TRUST HIM WITH ALL MY HEART.

PSALM 28:7

IN HIM WE HAVE REDEMPTION THROUGH HIS BLOOD, THE FORGIVENESS OF SINS, IN ACCORDANCE WITH THE RICHES OF GOD'S GRACE.

EPHESIANS 1:7

I TRUST IN YOUR UNFAILING LOVE. I WILL REJOICE
BECAUSE YOU HAVE RESCUED ME. I WILL SING TO
THE LORD BECAUSE HE IS GOOD TO ME.

PSALM 13:5-6

WALK IN THE WAY OF LOVE, JUST AS CHRIST LOVED US AND GAVE HIMSELF UP FOR US AS A FRAGRANT OFFERING AND SACRIFICE TO GOD.

EPHESIANS 5:2

"YOU WILL CALL ON ME AND COME AND PRAY TO ME,
AND I WILL LISTEN TO YOU. YOU WILL SEEK ME AND FIND
ME WHEN YOU SEEK ME WITH ALL YOUR HEART."

JEREMIAH 29:12-13

MY SOUL FINDS REST IN GOD;
MY SALVATION COMES FROM HIM.

PSALM 62:1